eat.

eat.shop.vancouver. *first edition*

Vancouver is a city of freewheelers. Of course, we work as hard as anyone, but we love to laze, to loll and luxuriate in the afternoon sun, or the early morning rain. Though the landscape often vies for our attention, we also revel in the smallest details that define our City: a favourite neighbourhood bistro, that fantastic sushi place or coffee bar. It is in these details that we have found a place to belong.

So too have Nick and I found our niche. The eat.shop. series was conceived of by our friend Kaie Wellman who champions small, community businesses in the same way that we do. Where better to purchase fresh dungeness crab than your local fish monger? Or freshly baked bread and sweet cupcakes than a local baker and patisserie? In this day of homogeneous shops and restaurants, that the little guy survives at all qualifies, almost, as miraculous; that the ones celebrated here are giddily thriving is a testament to taste.

In Vancouver we are fortunate enough to have access to a plethora of mutlicultural food and wine. Vancouverites clamour for French bistros, sushi counters, Indian eateries, Irish pubs and superb chocolatiers—thankfully all of these are in abundance. Not to mention the expanse of shops and boutiques that exhibit handcrafted furniture, local designers and artisans and imported fineries of all description.

This guide is, by design, a highly personal litany of retailers and restaurateurs. It is a compilation of mine and Nick's favourite stops. It is not meant to be comprehensive, but rather a wabi sabi of places and things that we love. In other words, our list of things slightly imperfect, modest and unconventional, but wholly invaluable. No doubt we have missed a few finds (so please let us know). However incomplete, this guide tries to offer a certain truth: contained within are the people and the places whose whets and wares have touched us, and shaped a nice little part of our lives.

Sophia LaDouceur
08 September 2004

our top twenty eating experiences in vancouver

sophia:

the wait at vij's
shrimp and avocado salad at trafalgars
parkside's seasonal cherry crush
at waazubee, stephen's irrepressible hospitality
raspberry tango from chocolate arts
wild rice's hot and sour squid soup
back-lit bamboo bar at tangerine
big bowls of latte à la sophie's
terra bread's piping hot tomato soup and cheese croutons
lesley stowe's smoked trout mousse

nick:

salmon burger platter at moderne burger (with a cherry lime soda)
laughing it up with bartender steve at the whip
hunting down the restaurants that serve storm's hurricane ipa
watching the alchemy of ramen broth at kintaro (then eating this alchemy)
pints of guinness at the irish heather
albacore tuna spring rolls at umami
blueberry flatbread at terra breads
sweet sixteen at cupcakes
streusel muffins at mix
sticky toffee pudding at the alibi room

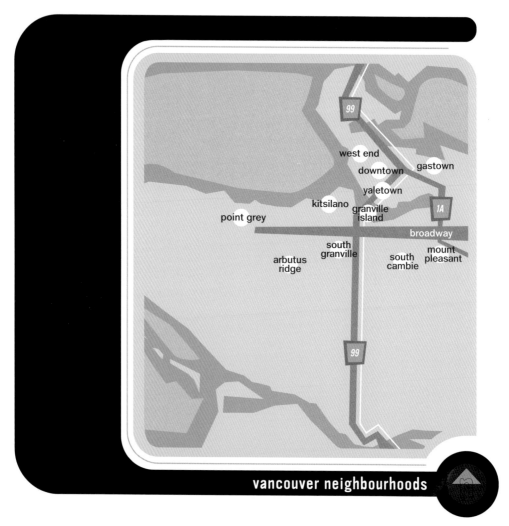

west end

downtown

gastown

yaletown

kitsilano

granville
island

point grey

broadway

south
granville

arbutus
ridge

south
cambie

mount
pleasant

99

1A

99

vancouver neighbourhoods

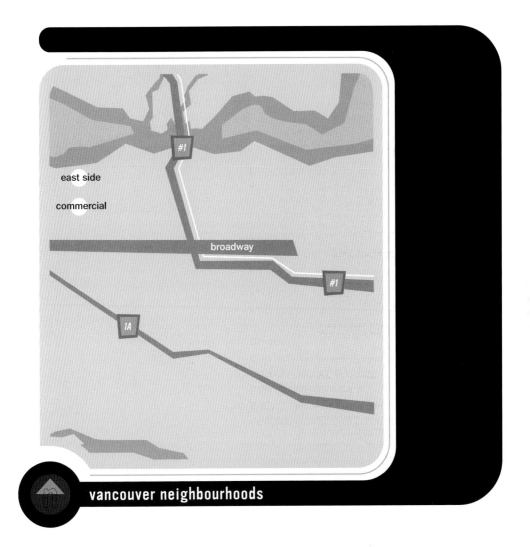

east side

commercial

broadway

#1

#1

1A

vancouver neighbourhoods

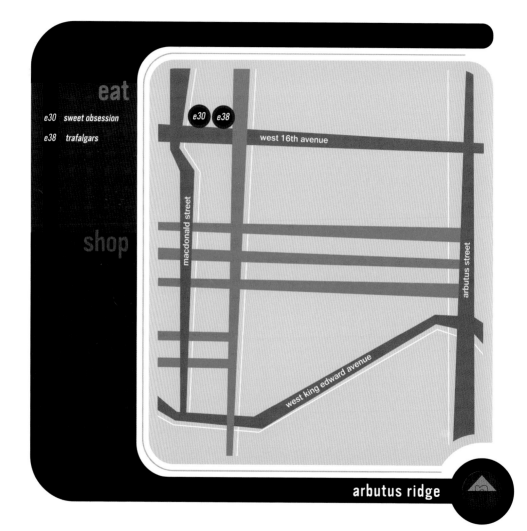

eat

e30 sweet obsession

e38 trafalgars

shop

west 16th avenue

macdonald street

arbutus street

west king edward avenue

arbutus ridge

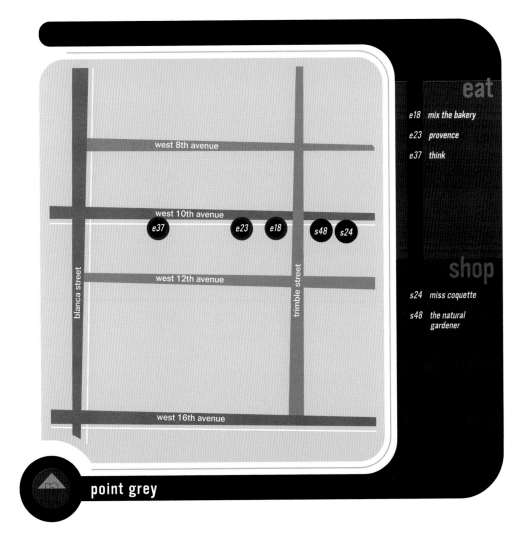

eat

e18 mix the bakery

e23 provence

e37 think

shop

s24 miss coquette

s48 the natural
     gardener

west 8th avenue

west 10th avenue

e37   e23 e18   s48 s24

west 12th avenue

west 16th avenue

blanca street

trimble street

point grey

eat

e3 baru latino

e11 fiction

shop

s10 garland's florist

s22 luna winters

kitsilano

eat

e2   arbutus real
     food market

e4   bistro pastis

e6   chocolate arts

e10 dan

e16 lesley stowe
     fine foods

e19 moderne burger

e27 sophie's cosmic
     cafe

e31 tangerine

e32 terra breads

shop

s4   bed

s19 kaya kaya

s33 readerwear

s36 robert held glass

s45 ta da!

kitsilano

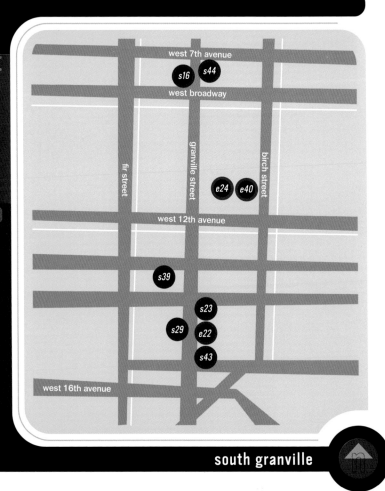

west 7th avenue

s16   s44

west broadway

granville street

fir street

birch street

e24   e40

west 12th avenue

s39

s23

s29   e22

s43

west 16th avenue

south granville

eat

shop

s20 lattimer gallery

s27 object design

s30 paper-ya

granville island

west end

downtown

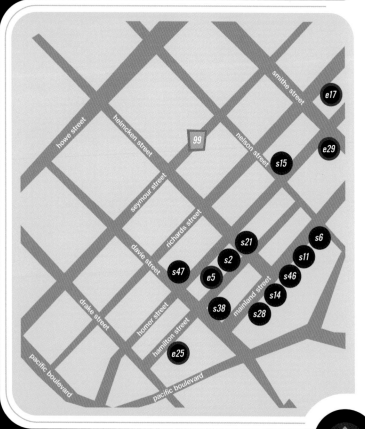

yaletown

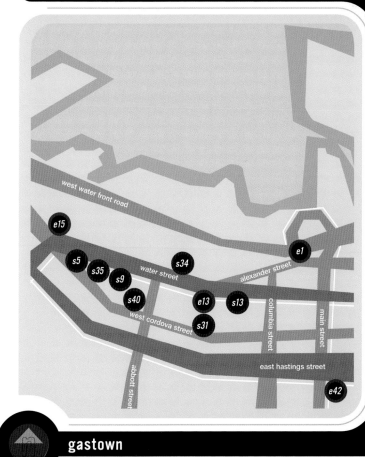

gastown

eat

e28 storm

shop

s12 gourmet warehouse

powell street

s12

e28

clark street

east hastings street

east pender street

frances street

commercial drive

east side

eat

e8   clove
e41   waazubee

shop

s7   chick pea
s8   doctor vigari
s42   spank

venables street

s42

napier street

grandview park

charles street

s8

commercial drive

e41

east 1st avenue

s7

e8

commercial

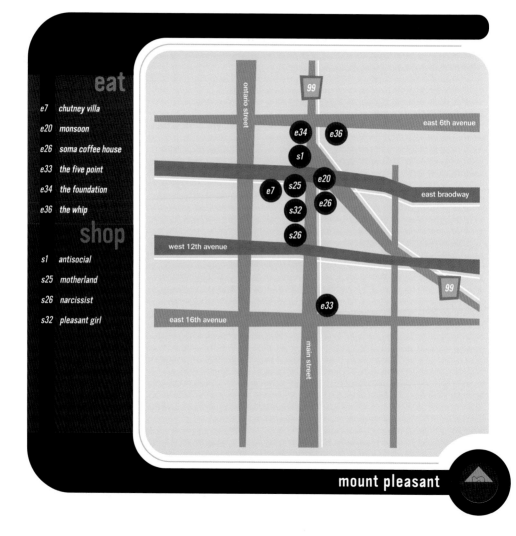

mount pleasant

west 16th avenue

cambie street

columbia street

s49

s17

west 19th avenue

douglas park

shop

ash street

west 22nd avenue

s17 jack

s49 woofgang

king edward avenue

eat

south cambie

alibi room

157 alexander street. corner of main and alexander
604 623 3383. www.alibi.ca. eat@alibi.ca
m – th. 5pm – close. fr. 4pm – 1am. sa. 10am – 1am. su. 10am – close

new global classic cuisine
opened in 1998
owners: rick stevenson, chris roberts and christian loubeck. chef: dean hillier
$$: mc. visa. debit
reservations recommended – not accepted for brunch

gastown > *e1*

for those who are unfamiliar with the edgy neighbourhood that is home to the alibi room, a trip to the "wrong side" of carrall street can feel adventurous. but this location has protected the alibi room from getting labeled as too trendy. never mind that this haunt's steady clientele is trendiness personified, an enclave of arty locals who work (or hope to) in music and film. upside: check out all the wrap parties.

imbibe:
dojo

devour:
tempura-battered stuffed tofu
pesto soba noodles
ever-changing daily fish special
macaroni & cheese with shrimp & rock crab
sticky toffee pudding

arbutus real food market

2200 arbutus street, corner of 6th and arbutus
604.736.5644 arbutusmarket@yahoo.ca
m - f: 6am - 7pm sa - su: 8am - 7pm

coffee shop
re-opened in 2002
owner: amanda rothgaber
$: cash only
reservations not required

kitsilano > **e2**

amanda found her destiny while caught in traffic on arbutus street a couple of years ago. contemplating a career change - she had managed a large bakery - she ended up stalled in front of the arbutus market, and two days later heard it was up for sale. now she makes great coffee and homemade pies for grateful neighbours. seems natural for a business that opened in 1907 as a sundries market for workers on the nearby rail lines.

imbibe:
italian sodas

devour:
honey granola muffins
homemade mixed berry & deep dish apple pies
classic french quiche
organic & fairly traded coffees

23

baru latino

2535 alma street. between broadway and west 10th
604.222.9171. www.baru.ca. baru@shaw.ca
mon-thu 5.30pm - 11.30pm. fri - sun 5.30pm - 1am

new latin cuisine
opened in 2001. chef: mark fremont
owners: carlos fonnegra, pablo rojas, nicole abusaid and camilo fonnegra
$$: mc. visa. debit
reservations not required

several months ago i discovered the very smokin' baru latino. well, at the time it felt like my discovery. the moment i boldly sauntered through the door, i was instantly struck by the crisp, high energy that proved to be as addictive as the stellar mojitos. intense reds and oranges permeated the space, the spice and the spirit. it felt as though the "cool kids" had finally invited me to sit at their table, only now they had citrus-laden ceviches and pisco sours instead of pb&j's.

imbibe:
mojito

devour:
cazuela baru aka caribbean bouillabaisse
guava glazed pork
octopus tiradito with black olive tapenade

so they say:
"The best mojitos in town..."

bistro pastis

2153 west 4th avenue. between arbutus and yew
604.731.5020 www.pastis.ca pastis@telus.net
lunch: tu - fr. 11:30am - 2pm brunch: sa - su. 11am - 2pm
dinner: tu - su. 5:30pm - 10:30pm

french bistro
opened in 1999. owner: john blakeley. chef: brad miller
$$$: all major credit cards accepted
reservations recommended

kitsilano > **e4**

ever since my first trip to paris, i have yearned for the bistro feel that imbued my visit. never mind the kir royale and bouillabaisse, it's the playful and intimate nature of a local haunt that i sorely miss. until pastis...a delightful bistro that almost (almost) eliminates the need to jet to france. precious few pleasures in life are more satisfying than sidling up to the bar at bistro pastis for an apéritif, an omelette du jour and a plate of salty pommes frites. finally...a bistro of my very own.

imbibe:
pastini

devour:
steak tartare
the french classic coq au vin
pan-seared dover sole

applause:
"Elegant French bistro with a lightness of being. A jewel."
- the vancouver sun

brix restaurant and wine bar

1138 homer street. between davie and helmcken
(604) 915-9463. www.brixvancouver.com. david@brixvancouver.com
tu - sa 16pm - 2am

pacifc northwest cuisine using regional ingredients
opened in 1998
owners: david hannay and patrick mercer. chef: jason wilson
$$: amex. mc. visa. debit
reservations recommended

yaletown > **e5**

this restaurant cum hotspot has lots of attitude, and whenever i enter the temptation is to do so with a flourish. it is blessed with that rare combination of a refined menu but a sexy, down-and-dirty air, and the setting is calculatingly casual setting. the scene here is every bit as good as the food; you need not stop elsewhere after dinner, because brix serves up a nightlife of its own.

imbibe:
over 60 wines by the glass

devour:
dungess crab cake
grilled wild b.c. salmon
tiger prawn bisque
warm quebec duck leg confit

applause
"The best restaurant is the one where they know me!"
- james beard

29

chocolate arts

westcoast-themed chocolate shop
opened in 1992. owners: patricia and greg hook
chef chocolatiers: greg hook and sarah cruickshank
$: amex. mc. visa

> **e6**

though I have been to chocolate arts *hundreds of times, i will never tire of its intoxicating scent or the artful display of its edible gems...not to mention the incredible chocolates that beckon from inside. these are chocolates that are meant to be savoured - held in your mouth until they slowly begin to melt and reveal the bewitching sweetness that lies within. indulge in a dark chocolate carmelita concealing an uber-rich, soft buttery caramel and you'll know what I mean.*

signature item:
haida medallions

devour:
madagascar truffle
rhubarb rhapsody
chocolate bowls filled with more chocolates

applause:
"This little Kitsilano store creates bonbons so beautiful and creative, you will want to put them on display...during thanksgiving you can sample a pumpkin-flavoured truffle...pure ecstasy." - yahoo travel

chutney villa

147 east broadway. corner of main and east. broadway
604.872.2228. chindi@yahoo.com
m. w. th. su (closed tu). 11:30am - 10pm. f + sa. 11:30am - 11pm

south indian cuisine
opened in 2003
owners: chindi varadarajulu and lisa lahey. chef: chindi varadarajulu
$-$$: mc. visa. debit
reservations not accepted

mount pleasant > **e7**

my incessant craving for hot, spicy food has finally met its match in the cuisine of southern india so expertly prepared at chutney villa. the highly habit-forming curries are laced with tangy tamarind, earthy cumin and ginger, rich coconut and a myriad of other flavourful elements. chindi and lisa will guide you through the menu, though even they can't explain one dish - chicken 65, tantalizing bits of chicken with fresh chiles and coriander so named for reasons no one can seem to recall.

imbibe:
masala chai

devour:
masala dosa
lamb prepared with a special blend of 7 spices
murtabak
biriyani

applause:
"Chutney Villa at Vancouver's epicentre of cool, puts a tangy twist on the vibrant cuisine of South India."
- the georgia straight

33

clove

735 denman street. between robson and alberni. 604.669.2421
2054 commercial drive. between 4th and 5th. 604.255.5550
denman: m - f. 5:30pm - 12am. sa. su. 5:30pm - 1am. bar open late
commercial: daily 5pm - close

tropical indian asian fusion
opened in 2000. owner: hsueh lin li. chef: martin scobie
$$: mc. visa. debit
reservations recommended

west end / commercial drive > **e8**

on one of the hottest days of one of the hottest summers ever (!), i was spared an untimely sidewalk expiration by the oasis that is clove. exhausted, delirious and without a moment to spare, i slipped into a cushy banquette and an icy glass of spicy spiced indian lemonade aka madras mukha. a team of paramedics could not have conceived of a better rescue than the clove kit of cocktail, curry and calm.

imbibe:
red ginger martini

devour:
thai cranberry duck
tuna ceviche
spicy coconut tofu
butter chicken

applause:
"Clove's menu items...are what other fusion restaurants should aspire to – an appreciative amalgamation of cultures, tastes and interpretation."
- pacific rim magazine

35

cupcakes by heather and lori

116 diana st. street (corner esplanade and pemberton)
604.974.1300 www.cupcakesonline.com cupcakes@telus.net
t.-fr. 10am – 11pm sa. – su. 10am – 12pm

cupcakes, cakes, brownies and cookies fresh baked daily from scratch
opened in 2002. owner/chefs: heather white and lori kliman
$: all major credit cards accepted
first come, first served

westside > **e9**

let everyone else bring over a nice bottle of wine when they attend a dinner party; now and then i show up with a rich batch of cupcakes. it's hard to walk by cupcakes, as eponymous as a business can be, and not succumb to a box of colourful sweetness. pink cupcakes, it turns out, can fix nearly everything. one day, no doubt, this will be clinically proven.

imbibe:
cold glass of milk

devour:
diva cupcake
cupcake wedding cakes
pink cupcakes t-shirts
party cakes - four vanilla or chocolate cakes
decorated in pastel colors

37

dan japanese restaurant

2511 west broadway, between larch and trafalgar
604.730.0308. tanromo@telus.net
sun. 5:30pm - 10pm. tue. - thu. 5pm - 10:30pm. fri. - sat. 5pm - 11:30pm

japanese
opened in 2003. owner: kenichi and tomoko oda. chef: kenichi oda
$$: all major credit cards accepted
reservations recommended

previous > e10

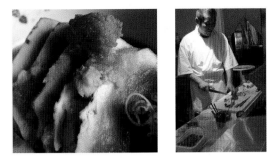

ken and tomoko designed dan to be as warm and welcoming as possible. walking into this new outpost in kitsilano is like walking into the home of an old friend for dinner. the sushi is beautiful here, culinary art as sustenance. a fusion of west coast and east asia spices and ingredients enlivens lovely fare-chopped prawn and scallop tempura; tuna sashimi infused with red chili. forgo the sake: here, you can have japanese vodka.

imbibe:
shochu (japanese vodka)

devour:
gindara saikyo yaki (grilled marinated sablefish)
dan kakiage (chopped prawn, scallop, &
japanese mint tempura)
dan special assorted sashimi
tuna chili sashimi

fiction

3162 Broadway. broadway between balaclava and trutch
604.736.7676
daily 5:30pm - 2am

wine country inspired bistro
opened in 1999. owner: sean sherwood
$$: mc. visa. dc. debit
reservations not required

kitsilano > **e11**

owner sean sherwood brings a downtown vibe to the after-work crowd in kitsilano, catering to foodies who can't bear to stay downtown for a good meal. in the heart of fleece and subaru land, fiction reads like something more chic. an icy-blue feel conjures up classier climes of the past. waiters pass by brandishing beef carpaccio, charcuterie by the platter, a house-ground okanagan beef burger. try pickup sticks-not some new dating game but a saucy new satay.

imbibe:
the kiss & the h²o

devour:
yam fries
pick up sticks
house cured charcuterie plate
valhrona chocolate taster

applause:
Social eating with wine country inspired cuisine.

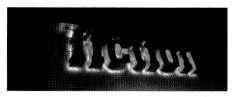

infuze tea house

670 west cordova street, corner of west cordova and howe
1014 denman street, corner of denman and pendrell
604 669 ... www.infuzeteahouse.com info@infuzeteahouse.com

__premium loose teas and tea enhanced beverages__
opened in 2002 $$: all major credit cards accepted
first come, first served

downtown / west end > e12

brian broke with family tradition. at age 12 he vowed never to join the family business, a lineage of tea masters stretching back a few centuries. he blames a rap on the knuckles that his grandmother gave him for breaking protocol when he entered the family tea room. he set out to find his own way, and infuze is the result. its plethora of eccentric concoctions of all sorts of teas would scandalize his ancestors. now infuze has expanded from its original site on cordova, opening a second outlet on denman-where i now acquire green tea lattes for a walk to the beach.

imbibe:
macha green tea latte
masala chili
iced burmese lime tea
rooibos vanilla latte
matcha green tea frappe

applause:
"The ultra-chic bar-style tea house is known for its premium blended tea beverages..."
- elle magazine

43

irish heather

217 carrall street. south of water street
604.688.9779 www.irishheather.com sean@irishheather.com
daily noon - 12am

authentic irish euro bistro
opened in 1993. owners: sean and erin heather
$-$$: amex. mc. visa
first come, first served

gastown > e13

if the irish heather *isn't the actual cornerstone of gastown, it surely anchors the area. until now, this irish pub has been a secret, and it holds a second one: through the courtyard in the back, there's a converted coach house with a red door and a determined-looking clientele. behind the door, sean has created the* shebeen, *and it's the sexiest room in town. it's cozy, it can be booked for special events and it has a wall lined with bottles of premium whiskey. what more could you want?*

imbibe:
guinness

devour:
bangers & mash
wild mushroom & feta strudel
blueberry & lemon curd bread pudding

applause:
"Highbrow food at low brow prices."
- the vancouver sun

kintaro ramen

788 denman street: north of robson at denman
604 682 7568
tu – su. noon 1 – 11pm

japanese ramen noodle soups
opened in 1999
owner: daiji matsubara. chef: daiji matsubara
$: cash. debit
first come, first served

> **e14**

ramen is an art. in the hands of kintaro's matsubara-san, it's an evolving masterpiece. a friend says kintaro serves the best ramen he has eaten outside of tokyo. at first i was skeptical, but then we imbibed, twice the first week and every week thereafter for a couple of months. it is a spare, unornate restaurant, where the focus is entirely on the ramen, a constantly evolving alchemy, in matsubara-san's view. i brought a homesick japanese friend to kintaro. she ate quietly, reverently, pausing halfway through to deliver a broad, sated smile. "soooooo good!"

imbibe:
beer

devour:
shoyu ramen
miso ramen
shio ramen
vegetable ramen

kitanoya guu

105-375 water street, corner of water and richards, 604.685.8682
888 thurlow street, corner of thurlow and robson, 604.685.8817
1698 robson street, corner of robson and denman, 604.685.8678
www.kitanoya.ca itosu@telus.net
gastown and west end: daily .5pm - 12am downtown: daily 11:30am - 12am

japanese izakaya stile (tapa)
opened in 1992 $$: all major credit cards accepted
reservations not required

gastown / central downtown / west end > e15

in a haven above the tourist-flooded streets of gastown, a favourite eatery thrives. at kitanoya guu, the food comes in streams of fascinating little dishes from masao, the chef. sometimes I am tempted to skip straight to dessert: tofu cheese cake.

imbibe:
green tea

devour:
aigamo (grilled duck breast w/ sweet soy sauce)
gindara (grilled black cod with saikyo miso sauce)
nanban (deep fried mackerel with sticky sauce)
hotate (baked scallops & mushrooms)

49

lesley stowe fine foods

1750 west 3rd avenue. corner of burrard and 3rd.
604.731.3663. www.lesleystowe.com
m-sa 9:30am - 6pm

contemporary north american cuisine with european and asian influences
opened in 1990. owner: lesley stowe. chef: juliana gola
pastry chef: eve lacabanne
$-$$: amex. mc. visa. debit
first come, first served

kitsilano > **e16**

lesley stowe *is a tasty stop halfway between my apartment and the granville island public market. on my way to gathering healthful produce and seafood, i often wander into* lesley stowe *and succumb to temptation: the handsome bottles of italian olive oil, waxed-paper packages concealing delicious aromatic cheeses, mustards married with every imaginable ingredient, rich chocolate desserts, savoury parmesan crisps... i mean, why fight it?*

signature item:
raincoast crisps

devour:
dungeness crab cakes with "real crab"- lots of it
grilled tuscan vegetables
chocolate caramel hazelnut mousse cake
caramelized fruit crostadas

lucy mae brown

862 richards street. richards near robson
604 899 9199. lucymaebrown@telus.net
open for dinner. 5:30pm – 2:30pm. tuesday – sunday. Bar to 2am.
lounge menu available from 2am

modern french with a nightclub vibe
opened in 2001. owners: sean sherwood, matt walsh, michael milton
chef: wolfgang reitshammer
$$: mc. visa. dc. debit
reservations recommended

> **e17**

sixty years ago lucy mae brown operated a bordello at this very address, or so local legend would have it. the bed-rooms and opium den no longer are in existence, but the air is still redolent of anonymity and sensuality. plush high-backed banquettes offer the perfect concealment for a discreet tete-a-tete. indulge in a delightful dinner or escape to the sexy, s-shaped lounge, accessible through a back alley door, for a "kiss" cocktail. or two.

imbibe:
mojito

devour:
tarte flambe
brochettes
salad winnipeg
veal carpaccio

so they say:
Downtown destination fine dining with high energy and high design.

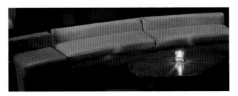

53

mix the bakery

4430 west 10th avenue. between sasamat and trimble
604.221.4145. p-nyberg@telus.net
daily. 7am - 6pm. f - sa until 10pm

artisan bakery

opened in 2003. owners: peter and rose nyberg. chef: thuy kelp
artisan baker: peter nyberg. pastry chef: rose nyberg
$: mc. visa
first come, first served

point grey village > **e18**

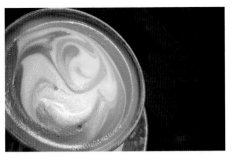

i guess it's probably evident that baked goods have a certain hold over me. peter and rose moved to town and managed to improve my life, all by making streusel muffins. i can't go near their neighbourhood without somehow finding myself wandering through the door of mix the bakery. i'll eat one here and then try to sneak a couple home for later. it's hard to avoid having to share the bounty; my satisfied grin always gives me away.

imbibe:
mexican hot chocolate

devour:
three chili cheese bread
chimayo chicken panini
triple ginger currant scone
chocolate oblivion

applause:
"Mix is about passion, on so many levels. Guaranteed to seduce...with its showcase of sensual pastries and racks of creative, crusty loaves."
- tim pawsey, the vancouver courier

moderne burger

2507 west broadway, corner of larch and west broadway
604 739 0005
daily noon - 9pm

classic burgers
opened in 2001
owners: peter and kathy
$: cash only
first come, first served

kitsilano > **e19**

this meaty joint came into being the hard way: it threw up a shiny new neon sign, posted a big "opening soon" banner and then languished for months as city workers went on strike. it was worth the wait: amazingly good burgers (try the salmon!) and fries and a dead simple menu. many of us in vancouver were frantic about when this new place would finally open up. now owners cathy and peter are like family for me.

imbibe:
chocolate malted milkshake

devour:
their homemade bbq sauce
sauteed mushrooms
fried onions
cheddar cheese burger

so they say:
"We are consistently reviewed as the top burger house."

57

monsoon east west brasserie

2526 main street. corner of broadway and main
604.879.4001. www.monsooneastwest.com
su - th: 5pm - 11pm. fr. sa: 5pm - 12am

regional asian fusion cuisine
opened in 1998
owners: ida cootauco, daragh steadman, kathryn thomson and seren kahlon
head chef: patrick lynch. sous chef: jason malloff
$$: amex. mc. visa. debit

mount pleasant > **e20**

this may the best date restaurant in town. for many folks it's a favourite in-the-city-getaway, and patrons promote it like they own a piece of the profits. for five years monsoon has served inspired asian cuisine to faithful customers from near and far. feast on duck confit, and savour palm-sugared bananas for dessert.

imbibe:
main street mango

devour:
braised lamb shank with tandoori mash
hoisin duck confit with scallion crêpes
steak salad with a cilantro, mint & lime dressing
chai brulée

applause:
"The Monsoon aesthetic is more than mere cultural excavation or global affectation. For many of the people who live in the neighbourhood, it's like home."
- vancouver magazine

59

parkside

1906 haro street. one block west of denman at gilford
604 683 6912. www.parksiderestaurant.ca. parkside@telus.net
daily 6pm - 12am

classically grounded cooking using local ingredients
opened in 2003. owner: chris stewart and andrey durbach. chef: andrey durbach
$$: mc. visa
reservations recommended

west end > **e21**

parkside truly is the idyllic all-season restaurant. in winter, the chilling, dogged rain is laughable from the warmth of the intimate dining room. in summer, the garden patio is heavily scented with the arresting fragrances of basil, sage and lemon thyme, which are masterfully folded into an ever-changing, deliciously seasonal menu. andre's discerning palate paired with chris's affable manner is an ideal combo, as rewarding as the glorious heirloom tomato salad bathed in aged balsamic.

imbibe:
bourbon sour

devour:
terrine of duck, potato & foie gras
veal sweetbreads with brown butter & capers
halibut fillet w/ wild mushrooms, onions & bacon

applause:
"The kitchen, which remains open until midnight, hosts plenty of industry folk late...They're the ones who know a bargain and respect the vision"
- jamie maw, food editor, vancouver magazine

picnic

3010 granville street. corner of 14th and granville
604.874.9412. www.picnicon.com
mon - sun. 5.30pm - 10.30pm. daily lunch specials.

asian fusion cuisine
opened in 2004. owner: linda meinhardt. chef: elke brandstadtatter
$$: amex. mc. visa. debit
reservations not required

okay, it doesn't get that cold in vancouver, not like churchill or montreal. but it does sometimes get a bone chilling dampness. it's kind of damp right now, and all i can think about is the hot cocoa from *picnic*. at first i didn't understand why this city deserved such an awesome cup of cocoa. now i'm not questioning it. sure the rest of the food is great for either eating at the huge picnic table at *picnic*, or for actually taking out. but right now, i really just want a cocoa.

imbibe:
hot cocoa

devour:
butter chicken
chocolate cherry cake
fresh salads

provence mediterranean grill

4478 west 10th street
604 222 1980 www.provencevancouver.com info@provencevancouver.com
dinner: m - th 11am - 10:30pm f - sa 11am - 11pm
brunch: sa - su 10am - 3pm afternoon tea: daily 2pm - 4:30pm

provençal inspired with west coast flare
owner: alessandra and jean-francis quaglia. chef: jean-francis quaglia
opened in 1997. $$: all major credit cards accepted
reservations required for dinner and afternoon tea

west point grey **>** **e23**

this restaurant is named for the place where alessandra and jean-francis met and fell in love. years ago i watched with fascination as they demonstrated how to prepare select dishes from jean-francis's native homeland. to this day i still make the pissaladiere garnished with salt-cured anchovies, black olives and sweet caramelized onions. the menu here is replete with delights from the mediterranean coast. settle in at a lovely windowside table, or take away neat, little containers of spicy lamb sausage with fennel and tomato or grilled squid tossed with lemons and chiles.

imbibe:
chef's martini or kir royale

devour:
bouillabaisse
prawns provencal
white chocolate & mixed berry clafoutis

applause:
"It's Mediterranean radiance warms the upper reaches of West 10th Avenue and is a welcome departure..."
- tim pawsey, the vancouver courier

65

rangoli

1488 west 11th street, corner of granville and 11th
604.736.5711   www.vijsrangoli.ca
daily 11am - 8pm

northern indian fusion
opened in 2004. owner/chef: vikram vij
$-$$: all major credit cards accepted
reservations not taken

one of the reasons i love rangoli *is the balance of flavours - sweet, salty, bitter and sour - that meld in perfect palatable harmony. at* rangoli, *the talented punjabi women who rule the kitchen ply piquant mint and coriander chutney, prepare sweet, mild raita from yoghurt daily, and flavour the fare with roasted cumin seeds and tart lemons.* rangoli *is the sister star of* vij's *though the atmosphere is sedate by comparison, the cuisine is no less exceptional.*

imbibe:
mango lassi

devour:
tamarind and yoghurt marinated grilled chicken
portobello mushroom and red bell pepper curry
vikram's own garam masala
wild salmon cakes.

rodney's oyster house

1228 hamilton street. between drake and davie
604.609.0080
m - th. 11:30am - 11pm. f. 11:30pm - 12am. sa. 1pm - 12am. su. 3pm - 10pm

simple ocean fare
opened in 1998. owners: stafford lumley and todd atkinson. chef: janet kis
$$: amex. mc. visa. canadian tire money
reservations recommended

yaletown > **e25**

wade into rodney's *almost any time of day and you're likely to find someone steeled behind the bar shucking oysters...always a good sign if it's freshness you're after. there are definite advantages to living in a coastal city - succulent dungeness crab and wild salmon are but two. the juicy menu celebrates fresh seafood in all its tantalizing forms - and if that weren't enough, rodney's makes a wicked vodka-laced caesar.*

imbibe:
zydeko stew

devour:
fresh, fresh oysters on the half-shell
hand-picked dungeness crab cakes
live atlantic lobster & dungeness crabs
freshly shucked pan-fried oysters

applause:
"Simple, fresh food in a casual setting."
- wguides.com 2004

69

soma coffee house & magazine store

2528 main street, off broadway at main
604-873-1750 www.somacafe.ca
daily 6am – 1 pm

coffee

opened in 1993. owners: jonathan kerridge and baven pillay
$: all major credit cards accepted
first come, first served

mount pleasant > **e26**

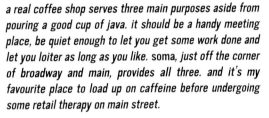

a real coffee shop serves three main purposes aside from pouring a good cup of java. it should be a handy meeting place, be quiet enough to let you get some work done and let you loiter as long as you like. soma, just off the corner of broadway and main, provides all three. and it's my favourite place to load up on caffeine before undergoing some retail therapy on main street.

imbibe:
handroasted milano coffee

devour:
lemon curd tart
full selection of sandwiches to grab & go
iced lattes
loose leaf teas

applause:
Best coffee shop in Vancouver 2003
- mia stainsbury, vancouver sun

sophie's cosmic cafe

2095 west 4th avenue. corner of arbutus and 4th
604.732.6810 www.sophiescosmiccafe.com
daily 8am - 9pm

traditional north american and eclectic cuisine
opened in 1988. owners: sophie, chris, jimmy and angela dikeakos
chefs: mike, kulsit, sherrie, kyle, lucky, adore and more
$-$$: mc. visa. debit
dinner reservations recommended for parties of 6 or more

kitsilano > **e27**

if you've been in town for all of 45 minutes you may already have heard about breakfast at sophie's cosmic cafe. it was my first breakfast stop when i moved here, and i have returned faithfully ever since. i usually ask for karen, the waitress who knows my order by heart: belgian waffles and a viet coffee. but sophie's is more than just a breakfast joint. it's also open for dinner...and you can get the waffles until five p.m.

imbibe:
real ice-cream shakes with booze

devour:
sante fe benny
kits lumberjack breakfast
burger platters
home-made veg & nut burger

73

storm brewery ltd.

310 commercial drive. commercial north of east hastings.
604 255 9119. www.stormbrewingvancouver.com
call for hours

rich character ales
opened in 1994. owner: james walton
$: cash or cheques

east side > **e28**

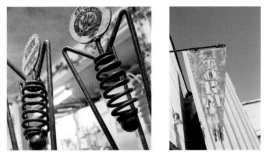

we know that this isn't eat.drink.vancouver, but we have included storm brewery because, frankly, we enjoy their beers. many of the excellent restaurants in this book serve storm beers; it's a good sign if an establishment has the wit to serve such a tasty beer. there isn't much to see at storm - they aren't really set up for tours or guests of any kind; but you can purchase a keg for your own consumption and who knows, they might just offer you a brew.

imbibe:
black plague stout
cherry lambic
echinacea ale
highland scottish ale

applause:
"a complex, flavourful and fascinating ale lies just on the edge of being totally out of control." - stephan beaumont, celebrator beer news on storm's hurricane IPA

subeez cafe

891 homer street, corner of smithe and homer
604.687.6107 www.subeez.com
m - f 11.30am - 1am sa - su 11am - 1am

casual west coast dining
opened in 1995. owner: benny deis. chef: rob and chi
$$: mc. visa
reservations recommended for groups of 8 or more

yaletown > **e29**

this restaurant is a great daytripper. cavernous and hulking, it is lined with soaring windows that let a flood of natural light bathe the concrete floors and pillars. at night, gothic towering candles suffuse the space in wavering illumination. a mélange of urbanites co-exists here, some sporting body hardware, others in pinstripes, still others balancing on jimmy choos. i like to share here, communing over subtle salads, satays and sides like tasty potstickers and tuna bites.

imbibe:
cosmo

devour:
garlic mayo fries
chicken & brie sandwich
cobb salad

so they say:
"Subeez is a contemporary West Coast cafe and restaurant with a cosmopolitan, urban atmosphere."

sweet obsession

2611 west 16th avenue. corner of trafalgar and 16th
604.739.0555. www.sweetobsessioncakes.com. info@sweetobsessioncakes.com
daily. 7am - close | 7am - 11pm. sa. 7am - 12am.

incredible desserts
opened in 1993
owners: lorne tyczenski and stephen greenham. chef: tracy kadanoff
$: amex. mc. visa. debit
first come, first served

arbutus ridge **>** **e30**

this dessert spin-off of trafalgar, the smallish bistro at the corner of west 16th and trafalgar avenue, was set to open as this book went to press. though it's a little off the main path, the sinfully scrumptious, always sumptuous desserts make the required meandering more than worthwhile.

signature item:
triple chocolate mousse

devour:
winter warm toffee pudding cake
summer fruit flan with fresh berries
fall deep-dish pumpkin pie with candied walnuts

applause:
"There is nothing as delectable as the aroma of freshly baked cakes and pies - unless it's the taste."
- customer

tangerine

1685 yew street, corner of 1st and yew
604.739.4677 www.tangerine.bc.ca
brunch: sa - su 9am - 2:30pm dinner: m - th 5pm - 11pm f - sa 5pm - late
may - april sunday dinner 5pm - 10pm

southeast asian and south pacific polynesian
opened in 1999. owners: wendy, janis & david nicolay, nigel pike & rob edmonds
chef: greg armstrong $$: all major credit and debit cards accepted
reservation recommended - not accepted for brunch

kitsilano > **e31**

since moving to this neighbourhood i too have succumbed to the addictive pastime known as weekend brunch. and i don't mean the early-risers' pancakes and sausages variety, (which admittedly has its merits), i mean the bleary-eyed, two-fisted kind with a peppery wasabi caesar in one hand and a steaming bowl of latte in the other. tuck into a hearty breakfast burrito, and sit back while nigel and wendy expertly mix the next round of eye-openers. hail caesar!

imbibe:
god of good and evil

devour:
macadamia crusted halibut
pineapple-chili sambal
spice rubbed lamb satay with masala mash
red coconut curried vegetables, chickpeas, tofu

applause:
"The bottom of Yew Street offers up the excellent Tangerine, where intelligently combined food, refracted through the prism of Asia, fills the modern space every night." - vancouver magazine

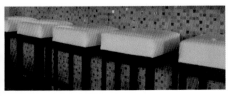

81

terra breads

2380 west 4th avenue. corner of balsam and west 4th. 604.736.1838
107 - 1689 johnston street. granville island public market. 604.685.3102
53 west 5th avenue. between ontario and manitoba. 604.873.8111
www.terrabreads.com mary.mackay@terrabreads.com
west 4th: daily 7am - 7pm. public market: daily 9am - 6pm west 5th: tbd

bakery and café specializing in artisinal breads and pastries
opened in 1993. owners: michael lansky, mary mackay. head baker: mary mackay
$: amex. mc. visa. debit

various neighborhoods > **e32**

one reason to never leave vancouver is terra breads. *more to the point, my family would never allow it. i'm often called upon to gather a cache of goodies to take home on whatever plane is jetting me across the country shortly after all orders are placed. baby apple cardamom cakes for mom, olive-studded loaves and fougasse for my sister, and for me, a scrumptious apple focaccia laced with warm, sweet caramel and a sprinkling of fresh thyme.*

imbibe:
terra's own lemonade

devour:
italian cheese loaf with parmesan & asiago
blueberry white chocolate flatbread
black mission fig & anise loaf
belgian chocolate brownies

applause:
Recipient of the "Best of Vancouver" Readers' Choice Award 8 years in a row. - the georgia straight

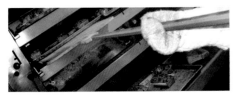

the five point

3124 main street. birwgin 16th and 18th
604.brwo18tu. www.thefivepoint.com
m-f 11am-2am. sat 9-11:30am. tue served brunch 10am-12pm

west coast casual
opened in 2003. owner: matt thompson
$-$$: all major credit cards accepted
reservations required only on weekends

sometimes a business opens in the right place at the right time. the five point - the "the" in the title apparently is required - is so blessed. as main street started finding its identity as an emerging bazaar for antiques and apparel, the five point opened as a place to hang out on the patio for a quick, tasty bite and something cold to drink. or a long, lingering conversation into the night, paced by several relaxing pints along the way.

imbibe:
something blue that chris the bartender makes that's delicious!

devour:
blackened tuna bites
vegetarian sushi rolls
lamb sirloin medallions
wild salmon filet

the foundation

2301 main street. corner of 7th and main
604.879.9663
daily. noon - 1am

vegetarian
opened in 2002
owners: mark thomson and amy woods. chef: mark thomson
$: mc. visa. debit
reservations are recommended for parties of 6 or more

mount pleasant > **e34**

this veggie-funk restaurant on main street used to be a secret jealously guarded by its first fans. they still whisper in hallowed tones when talking about it, but this eatery is no secret anymore. even beefeaters can savour the smoky, grilly tofu. the place simply rocks.

imbibe:
a storm brew

devour:
spicy peanut dish
east van town
molten tofu
sesame society

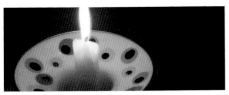

applause:
"...but no matter what you order, you'll feel like you're helping the cause somewhere." - the province

87

the templeton

1087 granville street. corner of helmcken and granville
604.685.4612 www.thetempleton.com thetempleton@telus.net
su - th 9am - 11pm f - sa 9am - 11am

gourmet diner classics

reopened in 1996. owners: jessica kaman and ricardo farinha
chef: jessica kaman, paris tubbs and jason zhao
$-$$: mc. visa. interac
first come, first served

downtown > **e35**

i love diners, and i love diner people. jessica and ricardo are paragons of this species. they used to eat at this spot, which has been a diner since 1934. a few years ago, when they heard it was going to be sold and gutted, they intervened and bought the place outright. now they run an efficient eatery that serves great food out of a scratch kitchen. no ostentation here. oh, and jessica is a boxer, so tip well.

imbibe:
any flavour of our $5 milkshake

devour:
portobello mushroom burger
grilled cheese sandwich
the trucker's breakfast
vegetarian lasagna

89

the whip gallery restaurant

209 east 6th: east 6th at main
604.874.4687 www.thewhip.ca info@thewhip.ca
m - f 11:30am - 1am sa 10am - 1am

unique menu of multicultural cuisine
owners: jonathan kerridge and kevin patrick chef: jon justice
$$: all major credit cards accepted
reservations accepted

mount pleasant > **e36**

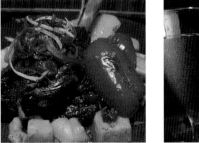

my australian cousin, pippa, took a sojourn in vancouver, and when she got here she ended up in this strange house on 6th near ontario. (not my fault.) when she complained that the area had nothing going on, i thought, "sure there is." so i walked her a couple of blocks up the road to the whip. a couple of pints and a plate of perogies later...problem solved. she became a regular for the rest of her duration here.

imbibe:
purple haze

devour:
goat cheese & focaccia crostini
salmon stuffed eggplant
braised lamb shanks
vegetarian pesto lasagna

think coffee lounge and bistro

4612 west 10th avenue. between tolmie and sasamat.
604 228 9510. thinkcl@telus.net
m - sa 7am - 11pm. su 8am - 10pm

speciality organic soups and sandwiches
opened in 2004
owner: greg lomnes. chef: jason brazeau
$: mc. visa. debit

point grey > **e37**

think *really is a place to think. greg envisioned this place when he was a student who liked to study in coffee shops but often wished he could grab a library book or two. his store now boasts a most impressive library... with beer on tap! that's my kind of study. and it's open late, injecting a little life into this charming but sleepy little strip.*

imbibe:
iced cognac espresso cooler

devour:
curried lentil soup with coconut milk
free-range turkey on cranberry walnut bread
wild smoked salmon on espresso dark rye
free-range chicken with green apples, tarragon

93

trafalgars bistro

2603 west 16th avenue. corner of trafalgar and 16th
604.739.0555. www.trafalgars.com. info@trafalgars.com
su - th: 9am - 10pm f - sa: 9am - 11pm

french-based west coast cuisine
opened in 1997
owners: lorne tyczenski and stephen greenham. chef: chris moran
$$: amex. mc. visa. debit
dinner reservations recommended – lunch reservations not accepted

arbutus ridge > **e38**

the epitome of a quiet neighbourhood bistro, trafalgars exudes a casual elegance that is an obvious extension of stephen's and lorne's good taste. the result is a convivial atmosphere, punctuated with enticing details: wood paneling, a dainty spray of fresh flowers, luscious libations... on my first visit i devoured a shrimp and avocado salad that is beyond compare. in fact the entire bistro-inspired menu is fresh and inventive. now that I know they're open for breakfast too, i may never have to cook again.

imbibe:
pousse rapière

devour:
poached eggs on potato latke with hollandaise
grilled chicken & brie panini
the risotto

applause:
"Trafalgar's is a quiet bistro with a patio nestled amongst burgeoning grape vines, two charming hosts and scrumptious seasonal dishes."
- grateful customer

umami tapas & wine

572 davie street. between richards and seymour
604.696.9563. umami@telus.net
m - th. 5:30pm - 12am. f - sa. 5:30pm - 1am. su. 5:30pm - 11pm

french, italian, spanish tapas with a twist of japanese
opened in 2003. owner: hiroshi shintaku. chef/sommelier: hiroshi shintaku
$$: amex. mc. visa
reservations are recommended

finding this tiny, jazzy tapas bar with a japanese twist is a happy experience. umami has a smart wine list, and the clever tapas are made by chef hiro shinataku. his creations will test your manners, for you will want to pick at everyone else's plate; at least try to confine this scavenging to the diners at your own table. the term umami means the fifth taste (after the four main ones: bitter, salty, sweet and sour). worry not, the dishes at umami will stroke all your other tastes buds as well.

imbibe:
blue heaven

devour:
albacore tuna spring rolls
gambas al ajillo
braised bbq eel with foie gras

applause:
"Simply because of its intelligent food and wine matches, in a city besieged by small plates, Umami takes tapas to the next level."
- tim pawsey, the vancouver courier

97

vij's

1480 west 11th avenue. northwest corner of granville
604 736.6664. www.vijs.ca. contact@vijs.ca
daily. 5.30pm - close

original seasonal indian cuisine
opened in 1994. owners: meeru and vikram vij. executive chef: vikram vij
$$-$$$: amex. mc. visa
first come, first served

south granville > *e40*

vikram is a proud restaurateur who dotes on his customers as though they were guests in his own home. that comfortable informality lends itself to a deliciously sensual evening. though he strongly adheres to a first come first served ethos that often creates lengthy queues, the worst that will happen is down time with a tall, frosty glass of cold beer in a cozy lounge or amidst bamboo fronds beneath a sinking sun. trays of lightly salted, piquant deep-fried mogo and fluffy naan nestling sweet mango chutney appear just often enough to whet your appetite. for once, luxuriate in the wait.

imbibe:
ginger-lemon

vikram likes:
sated diners

applause:
"Easily among the finest Indian restaurants in the world."
- the new york times

waazubee

1622 commercial drive. between first and grandview
604-253-5299. waazubee@pacificcoast.net
daily 11:30am - 1am

eclectic café
opened in 1993. owner: benny deiss. chef: andré tremblay
$-$$: mc. visa
reservations not required

commercial drive **>** **e41**

this spacious nouveau bistro fits right in amongst the motley crew of businesses on commercial drive and their even more motley assortment of patrons - willful, singular, difficult to define. the food here is accompanied by unusual artwork. prehistoric birds fashioned out of metal and strung from the skylight hover over the center of the room. the food is a comfort; the mashed sweet potatoes with bourbon and truffle oil are yummy.

imbibe:
lychee lemongrass martini

devour:
creative seafood dishes, such as 3-chipotle fish
sweet potato bourbon truffle mash
modern/classic cocktails per london, aussie bars
the famous garlic mayo fries

applause:
"Best gin list in British Columbia."
- jurgen gothe, cbc radio

wild rice

117 west pender street. between cambie and beatty
604.642.2882. www.wildricevancouver.com. apong@wildricevancouver.com
mon to thurs 11.30-11. fri 11.30-12. sat 5-12. sun 5-10

modern chinese
opened in 2001
owners: andrew wong, terri storey and tom poirier. chef: stuart irving
$$: mc. visa. debit
first come, first served

where gastown and chinatown meet > *e42*

shop.

eat.shop.vancouver. *first edition*

Like many Vancouver residents, I'm originally from somewhere else. And like many other transplants I've had friends, acquaintances and family come to visit. Or ask for advice on what to do while in Vancouver – a question that I used to dread. It's difficult to satisfy everyone, especially since some guests are higher maintenance than others. I could suggest touring around Stanley Park, or hiking up Grouse Mountain, visiting the local museums and galleries, but there's so much more to do than that.

So I started making mental notes on what's interesting, and what's happening in this city. I wanted to be prepared for the next time a guest came and asked me where they should eat, or where to shop. For the most part it works. And if you do it right, it's fun to join them on their explorations.

Like most people, we became accustomed to keeping mental lists of what to do with this guest or that guest. We welcomed the chance to formalize it in print.

To echo the sentiment of the series creator, Kaie Wellman, there are two main pleasures in compiling a book such as this: one is touring around, meeting people, and seeing how vital some neighbourhoods have become; the other is getting to share a fascinating city, that was once considered sleepy, but blessed with easy weather.

But a big part of the pleasure of this project has been rediscovering Vancouver. Either by getting tips from the people that I've met ("Have you tried this place?", "Have you checked out our neighbour? They're doing some cool stuff."), or just happening into a store because it's on the way to another.

We did a lot of this on foot. A slower pace means you're not whisked past a something that might be a real find. So we hope that our choices are invaluable and easy to find, even if you don't have a car. We've also tried to make useful clusters of businesses in areas that are subtly or sometimes dramatically different, one from the other. That's been part of the fun.

Nick Heron
08 september 2004

our top twenty shopping experiences in vancouver

nick:

gorgeous porcelain at kaya kaya
anything of ross' at industrial artifacts
surface to air at pigeon
tsubo shoes at intra-venus
pink shirt at vasanji
chinese medicine cabinet at jacana
my recently purchased norf london t-shirt at motherland
vinyl at room 430, plus joking with dawn
serge lesage carpets at spiral living
indulging my inner magpie at roost

sophia:

at dream, wendy's effervescent personality
the fromage sidetable at smalllmediumllarge
candy jars filled with lustrous gold and orange canoli-shaped shells from the cross
jack spade satchel at richard kidd
anything, or rather, everything from paper-ya
lattimer gallery's moss green and black harris smith maple plate
panties with pockets at luna winters
watching the firey art of glassblowing at robert glass' studio
apricot bridal gown at something blue
gourmet warehouse's paella pans

antisocial

skateboard shop and gallery
opened in 2002. owners: rick mccrank and michelle pezel
mc. visa. debit
street market sale one night only in august

> **s1**

antisocial *purports to be a skateboard shop, but the floor space here is so sweeping and bare that it feels almost like a latter day roller rink. i defy you to avoid the urge to grab a board and start cruising around indoors. when you're done wheeling around out front, check out the great gallery in back. so many coffee shops and restaurants are adding them that it borders on the cliche, yet the gallery here actually makes sense. design and art meld with all things skating, and this is a chance to see what the artists do on their own time.*

covet:
crownfarmer tees - bob k. is #1
girl and chocolate skateboards
hamber eyes' art prostitute and artkitip magazines
van slip-ons and sk8 highs
many, many skateboards and other fun things

babe belangere boutique

classic and chic women's clothing and accessories
opened in 2001. owner: tania sevierin
amex. mc. visa. debit

> **s2**

a perky outpost among the lofts and warehouses of yale-town, babe belangere *offers a wardrobe of trendy, flirty outfits for any woman who wants to rock a look that is both playful and sexy. if you're so inclined, round out your look with wispy lingerie and irresistibly cute flip-flops. in this darling boutique, sexy often wins.*

covet:
isabella fiore beaded and brocade handbags
seven jeans with pink swarovski crystal pockets
red silk marilyn monroe dress
nougat london multicolour tweed coat
chunky metal jewelry from paris
french kitty "breakfast at tiffany's" tees

so they say:
"Fashion changes, style remains."
- coco chanel

beautymark

beauty apothecary
opened in 2001. owner: marc brunet
amex. mc. visa. debit. traveler's cheque

> **s3**

i must confess i am an easy mark when it comes to pack-aging. if it were carefully wrapped in gorgeous paper and tied-up with string, a plastic container of tictacs would suddenly seem to me like the purchase of a lifetime. at beautymark *the packages are as pretty as the results promised by their contents - how did i survive this long without a frosted glass jar of honey face scrub, or a bronze cylindrical tube of nude gloss – i may never know.*

covet:
fresh
bumble and bumble
bliss
cargo
paula dorf
deluxe beauty

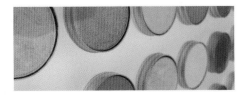

applause:
"A trove of beauty products awaits at this laid-back boutique, a favorite of some of the many actors (Bridget Fonda, Angie Harmon) who frequent Vancouver during movie shoots." - lucky.

bed

bedding
opened in 1999. owner: david
amex. mc. visa. debit
semi-annual "mistint" sale

>

face it, you need new bedding. what you've got is probably a little old and a little drab. at a monument to sleep that is known simply as bed, the drab gives way to a niagra falls of fun and splashy colours. have fun matching up a new set for yourself or for someone in need of a burst of brightness in her life. my family is no longer surprised when they get new sheets for christmas and birthdays.

covet:
cotton muslin bedding in over 50 solid colours
bed's racing stripe duvet covers
bed's ever-changing selection of graphic prints
100% cotton corduroy duvet covers

block

women's and men's clothing and accessories
opened in 1999. owners: isabelle dunlop and jennifer mackay
amex. mc. visa. debit. traveler's cheque
boxing day sale and summer sale in late july

so many valuable shopping hours have been squandered in my hunt for the perfect printed tee that i simply stopped searching. why bother? all the hype about the great fit, the understated design, the sensational colour...a cunning urban fashion myth propagated by desperate retailers. resigned to a life of basic black, i suddenly was proven wrong. jennifer and isabelle have lined the shelves of block with fantastic printed t-shirts that wear stylishly – and fit to a tee.

covet:
exclusive isabelle dunlop shawls & ponchos
fillipak brightly coloured sweaters
lacoste polos for men & women
built by wendy of new york city
fabulous denim
montréal designer philip dubuc's tailored couture

13

boutique vasanji

contemporary clothing, shoes and accessories for men and women
opened in 1990. owner: raz vasanji
amex. mc. visa. debit. traveler's cheque

> *s6*

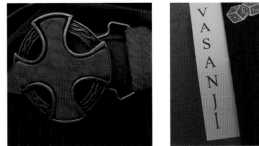

yaletown's claim to cool was bound to happen sooner or later, but it was clinched when boutique vasanji *relocated here from kitsilano. it's like a gallery, featuring sexy, upscale euro-looks. the clothes here are so well selected that they seem tailored, in advance, just for you. the big names are here, but i like to watch for the unexpected designs from the looms of london, turkey and italy. you'll be moved to know you can look good in something you hadn't considered before. go ahead - try it on.*

covet:
saskia as flora scarves & ponchos
custo barcelona
parasuco jeans
tribal alliance handcrafted australian trucker hats
lisa bodnaruk's woodever
tween clothing for men

applause:
"Colorful and vibrant treasures for your home." - press

15

chick pea

children's boutique
opened in 2004. owner: sarah hoivik
mc. visa. debit
semi-annual tea party

> **s7**

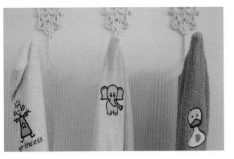

this children's boutique is as quiet and lovely as blue-eyed sara herself, and it brims with sweet bits and pieces that can make you wish your "tween" was a toddler again. not long after walking in, i tried to conceive of a way to go back in time so my precious nieces and nephews could still make use of such irresistible items as a charming bib freckled with bubblegum-coloured poodles. maybe baby goodies no longer apply, but who couldn't use a soft, hooded towel? even one with giant, green frogs.

covet:
olive & scarlett
schylling cowboy alarm clock
lolo's jewellery for children & mama's
eeboo good habits chart
tea collection
bebe fermier knitwear from brazil

applause:
"Colorful and vibrant treasures for your home."

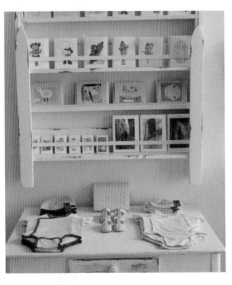

17

doctor vigari

15 Commercial Drive, between charles and kitchener
604 255 9513. www.doctorvigarigallery.com
tues to sat 11am to 6pm. sun 12pm to 5pm

gallery featuring a variety of talented local bc and canadian artists
opened in 1991. owner: bill gotts
all major credit cards accepted

> *s8*

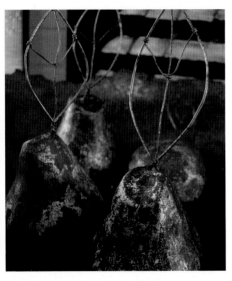

even bill has a really hard time trying to classify doctor vigari *(but then, i have an equally hard time trying to categorize some of my favourite vancouverites). suffice it to say this place offers iconoclastic gifts for iconoclastic people, the ones who are always so hard to match with just the right present. better yet, buy something for yourself...handpainted marble coasters, fine ceramics with the texture of a kitten's tongue, or perhaps long-stemmed steel roses.*

covet:
red bug bijoux jewelry
paintings by cindy moore
sculpture by ken clark
fantasy furniture from izabella beaumont
sculptural furniture by straightline design
industrial furniture by slightly bent design

DOCTOR vigari
GALLERY
604-255-9513

dream

311 w cordova street, between homer and hamilton
604.608.2660 dream@portal.ca
m . tu . 11am - 6pm w . th . 10:30am - 6pm f . 10:30am - 7pm
sa . 10:30am - 6pm su . 1pm-6pm

98% pure vancouver-made contemporary clothing and accessories
opened in 1993. owner: wendy de kruyff
amex. mc. visa. debit. jcb

gastown >

on the fringe of gastown, **dream** *is a fun girl's playhouse. it's filled with funky finery to dress yourself from head to toe. wendy, gregarious and disarmingly approachable, showcases a rare collection of creations from hundreds of on-the-rise vancouver designers. i still yearn for that stylish green wool surtout.*

covet:

multidisk rings by see:be
anything by dust
anything by allison wonderland
norie's canvas bags
suzanne cowan's handmade books
lustre mismatched earrings designed by devon

garland's florist

florist
opened in 1996. owner: aniko kovacs
all major credit cards accepted

> **s10**

flowers are so evanescent they are almost wasteful - so pretty but so pricey and short-lived. then i walk by garlands florist on broadway and become enthralled by the scent and flash of a platoon of bursting bouquets, and it dawns on me: flowers are a necessary ingredient in happiness. i can't remember the last time i actually planned to buy flowers, but everytime i steer myself inside i buy more than i'd ever expected. these days my house is so often stocked with a fresh bunch that friends ask me if it's for a special occasion. umm... it's tuesday!?

covet:
seasonal posies and pave's
european hand-tied bouquets
orchids from singapore
tropical foliages from peru
garden accessories

so they say:
"...candy store for the flower-obsessed, and a place for people who are passionate about funky, modern, sophisti-cated flower design."

23

global atomic designs inc

1006 main ave. street. between michael and michael
604 606 6223. www.globalatomic.com. info@globalatomic.com
summer hrs. sa - th 10am - 7pm su noon - 6pm
winter hrs. 11:30am - 8pm

fashion boutique
opened in 1998. owner: astrid fox
mc. visa. debit

> **s11**

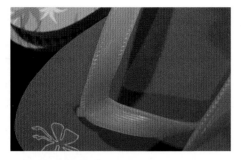

astrid has always been a discerning shopper - so discerning that she could rarely find the offbeat brands and objects she was looking for. she started global atomic designs to stock the elusive wares she couldn't find elsewhere. the resulting avalanche of objets, from lesser known but highly talented purveyors, warrant a thorough sifting in search of treasures you never knew you desired. but this time, they were found. well done.

covet:
one of a kind adidas originals
european & american premium denim
eclectic local labels
nixon watches

gourmet warehouse inc

gourmet food, housewares, bath, books
opened in 1978. owner: caren mcsherry
mc. visa. debit

> **s12**

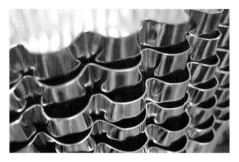

this store is steeped in culinary eye-candy. every imaginable vessel from paella pans to copper skillets is available here, joined by the artillery to use in them - silicone brushes, olivewood spoons, cookbooks, serving platters and glassware. oodles of delicacies are here, too - russian caviar, bars of bittersweet chocolate and anchovy sauce (believe me your life will be better for it).

covet:
aged balsamics - 8, 10, 12 & 15 years old
the finest chocolate from all corners of the globe
russian caviar
unfiltered olive oil from italy
professional non-stick pans
vast selection of salts & pepper rubs

industrial artifacts

49 powell street 1/2 block east of Gastown k
604.874.7797 www.industrialartifacts.com ross@industrialartifacts.com
open by appointment w – sat noon – 6pm. sun noon – 5pm

one of a kind furniture, art and design
opened in 1998. owner: ross macmillan
amex. mc. visa. debit

previous > **s13**

if you stroll the streets of gastown, you still risk missing industrial artifacts, tucked away in a spot just past the tourist district, mere meters beyond the statue of gassy jack. it's a showroom for fantastic objects from another era that have been reconfigured, emerging as unique furniture and art. this is the fate of old stuff that is lucky enough to find its way into the hands of ross macmillan...if you're lucky enough, some of it will find its way into your home.

covet:
the 'blade' coffee table
sprocket and gear-patterned mirrors
rocco's boxes & 'screws' chair
blueprint coasters designed by ross
the autopsy table
'alien landing' chandelier

applause:
"Ross MacMillan makes hunky, handsome furniture from recycled industrial components...hand-carved cedar, pine, maple, mahogany, and fir." - Wallpaper Magazine

29

intra-venus

072 hamby street. corner of hamilton and drake st
604.687.6969. www.intra-venus.com. info@intra-venus.com
m-w-sa: 11am - 6pm. th: 11am - 7pm. f: 11am - 8pm. su: noon-5pm

unique footwear and handbags
opened in 1998. owner: troy cruickshank
amex. mc. visa. debit. traveler's cheque
surprise! colour-themed sales

yaletown > s14

for shoe addicts in need of an intervention, intra-venus is unashamedly overflowing with temptations. it's only a hole in the wall, but for sole-full fanatics the place is part temple, part emporium. if you're going to indulge your habit, do it well.

covet:
a fun pair of camper twins
lacoste shoes for boys & girls
lovely & wicked miss sixty heels
puma nuala
cydwoqs

31

islands home collections ltd

901 homer street, corner of smithe
604.676.1627 www.islandshc.com mnicholas@islandshc.com
m - f 11am - 7pm sa 10am - 6pm su noon - 5pm

furniture, home décor and gifts
opened in 2002. owner: michael nicholas
amex. mc. visa. debit
teak garden sale in may, june and july

yaletown **>** *s15*

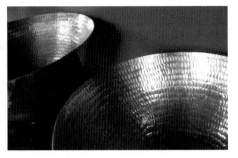

if trekking to asia is sometimes too daunting, consider a trip to islands instead. michael spent years of study and consultation in southeast asia and france, and it shows up in the cross-cultural mix of asian and european designs he has assembled at islands: rare teak furniture, flawless turned wooden bowls in polished shades of milk and dark chocolate, plantation chairs perfect for lounging. my temperature rises whenever i linger here, warmed by the rich red hues of cayenne, paprika, clove and cinnamon that imbue some of the treasures on display.

covet:
rustic tables in teak salvaged from old buildings
water hyacinth & abaca sofa sets
leather easy chair & footstool
plantation teak garden furniture
asian vases & bowls in natural materials
candles & incense in natural fragrances

33

jacana

2420 granville street. between broadway and 8th avenue
604.871.9050 www.jacanagallery.com closed monday. tuesday –
friday 11am – 6pm. sat 11am – 6pm

fusion of unique asian antiques and contemporary art and accessories
opened in 1999. owners: dany filion and peng liu
amex. mc. visa. debit

i want to live at the store that dany and her husband have created. they import ancient antiques that he unearths in china and refinishes, refurbishes and ships to vancouver. but jacana boasts a mix of contemporary art, too...i adore the timeless chinese hutch.

covet:
the jacana collection of porcelain lamps
zoë's wool & silk tibetan rugs
chinese antique chairs
indonesian ceremonial masks
alex's carvings & paintings
jewellery designed by qing qing

so they say:
"We buy objets d'art from all parts of the world and we ship objets d'art to all parts of the world!"

jack

3386 cambie street. between 17th and 18th
604.874.5225. www.jackhair.com. info@jackhair.com
m-th 10am - 8pm f. 10am - 7pm sa. 9am - 7pm

the modern barbershop
opened in 2003. owner: neil barkey aka jack
mc. visa. debit

this newfangled, self-consciously masculine hair salon offers tech for your head: a waiting area that boasts flat-screen tv's that occupy an entire corner, and a so-slick mac at the ready. catering to the boy in all men, this place seats them in funky orange chairs that look as though they were plucked from a stadium. the stylists here are utterly beautiful - women only, natch.

covet:
hair consultation to update the do
mvp treatment
satellite televisions at every station
x-box & high-speed internet while you wait
american crew

applause:
"I watch tv while getting my hair cut, my girlfriend loves my new look...I love this place!" - loyal customer

37

jeweliette

692 seymour street. corner of west georgia and seymour
604.687.5577. www.jeweliette.com. jeweliette@canada.com
m - sa. 10:30am - 6pm

fashion jewellery
opened in 1981. owner: madalena corsi
amex. mc. visa. debit. dc

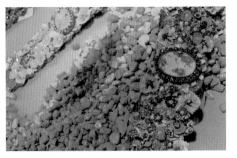

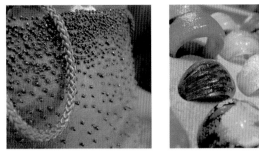

it is truly a pleasure to stumble into jeweliette, a gem in an otherwise uninspired cluster of offices and retail shops. madalena and her daughter elsa (jeweler to the stars) conspire to bejewel the city, suburbanites and sophisticates alike. wandering through the store, chunky rings in iridescent shades of coral, aqua and burnt orange called out to me. and soft, satiny evening bags are a lovely lure even for me, someone who balks at the idea of carrying a purse at all.

covet:
elsa corsi's crystal retro-inspired brooches
organza flowers by allison price
delicate creations in swarovski crystal by twinkle
elegant cocktail rings
earrings worthy of any red carpet

so she says:
"More is more, less is a bore!"

39

kaya kaya

2030 west 4th avenue. between a burns and maple
604-732-1816
m - sa 10am - 6pm. su noon - 5pm

japanese porcelain and traditional crafts
opened in 1978. owner: michiko sakata
amex. mc. visa. debit

kitsilano > **s19**

i'm forever grateful to michiko sakata for bringing the best of japan to vancouver via kaya kaya. she handpicks the delicate sake servers, tea and sushi sets and unusual glassware that fill the shop. i adore the gorgeous, colourful porcelain dishes that gleam from every corner. you won't want to leave empty-handed...wooden or lacquer chopsticks and hand-painted chinese zodiac cards (eerily accurate and frame-worthy) make perfect souvenirs or stocking stuffers – just ask my family.

covet:
clay raku pottery containers by mas funo
one-of-a-kind japanese silk kimonos
decorative, hand-painted cards by dan yan hu
traditional jyubako boxes
white porcelain dishes

41

lattimer gallery

1590 west 2nd avenue. between fir and west 2nd

northwest coast native art gallery
opened in 1986. owner: peter lattimer
amex. mc. visa. debit. dc

> *s20*

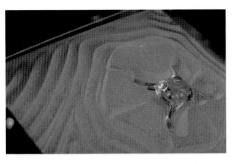

the pieces are emphatically one-of-a-kind at lattimer gallery, *and delightful surprises spill from the walls. smooth and spiky masks in bold colours. curio-cabinet sculptures of primitive, inukshuks (totem-like stone markers used hundreds of years ago by the inuit). my favourite: traditional bent boxes so named because they are created from a single piece of wood that is steamed and then bent into shape.*

covet:
native jewellery in sterling silver & gold
unique collection of steam-bent boxes
limited edition prints & original paintings
hand-carved wood sculptures

about:
"The partnership between the artists and the gallery make it what it is."

43

lola

1076 hamilton street. between helmcken and nelson
604 633 5017
m–f 11am – 6pm. sa 10am – 6pm. su noon – 5pm

home and apparel
opened in 2001. owners: christina mcdaniel and sue evans
amex. mc. visa. debit

yaletown > **s21**

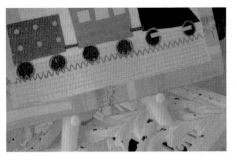

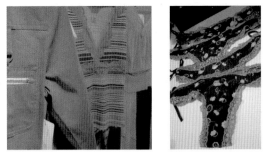

this artful "lifestyle boutique" has a distinctly parisian feel, complemented by a british eccentricity. christina and sue have assembled a panoply of soaps, scents and accessories that conspire to make you feel good. lilac sachets, tiny burberry baby bunting, polka-dotted neckrolls, vintage china and silverplated tea sets: go ahead, indulge yourself.

covet:
burberry baby
my flat in london handbags
only hearts lingerie
jewellery by queen bee
diptyque candles & fragrances
juicy couture kids

applause:
"Lola is a girl's dream come true...mcdaniel's european influences definitely shine through at this gorgeous little lifestyle store." - fashion.

45

luna winters

3070 west broadway. between balaclava and bayswater
604.738.7305. www.lunawinters.com. mara@lunawinters.com
m - sa 10am - 6pm. f 10am - 7pm. su noon - 5pm

children's lifestyle boutique
opened in 2004. owner: mara maldonado
mc. visa. debit
winter sale on boxing day through january and summer sale in july and august

kitsilano > **s22**

why didn't they sell this stuff back when i was girl with a curl? this store is imbued with brilliant autumnal and summer colours, splayed over imaginative and playful children's wear. to wit: adorable little panties adorned with pockets, something i still could really use. and kid-sized panchos with a spanish flair, laid out in an exotic mix of oranges, reds and mustards cooled by ocean blues and citron yellows.

covet:
fingerpaint soap for bathtime
fuchsia baby girl shoes with bows
chalkboard t-shirts
handknit newborn caps with ears
pink faux fur jacket with matching booties
peaches & cream body lotion by skincandy

applause:
"Shopping for an impossibly chic tot? Steer your hot wheels over to Luna Winters."
- flare magazine

47

meinhardt fine foods

3002 granville street. corner of 14th and granville
604.732.4405 www.meinhardt.com
mo - sa 8am - 9pm su 9am - 9pm

gourmet food shop
opened in 1995. owner: linda meinhardt. chef: elke brandstadtatter
amex. mc. visa. debit

if there's one thing my sister natascha and i can agree on, it's our inexhaustible love for and fascination with gourmet food shops. years ago we fell prey to new york city's zabar's where we chose baskets full of goodies for an impromptu picnic in central park. since then, we have sought to recreate that experience. until now. meinhardt is chock-full of yummy delights for picnicking or stocking your pantry: triple-cream cheeses, french breads, grilled artichokes, gooey brownies, champagne vinegars, pastas imported from italy, chocolate and hazelnut spreads...to name a few, more or less.

covet:
our gift boxes
anything from our deli counter
anything from our catering department
our flower selection

so they say:
"All the basics, all the best."

49

miss coquette

lifestyle boutique
opened in 2003. owner: leanne dunic
mc. visa. debit

continued >

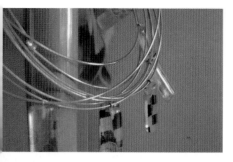
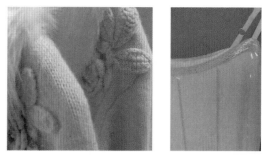

my senses fire up every time i launch myself into this sassy women's showplace. my eyes dance delightedly over an alluring mix of goodies in bright colours, geometric patterns and deconstructed shapes. leanne's own hand-knit pumpkin shrugs are on hand. the precious hand-painted silk bustiers, an eclectic collection of jewelry and indispensable books on "the art of cocktails" all could make for one lovely evening with someone deserving.

covet:
narcissist dresses by vancouver designer
naughty clothing from london
hawaiian colada, ice age, tiramisu rooibos teas
nanna's singular pieces made with recycled fabrics
damzels in this dress
reading bitter with baggage seeks same

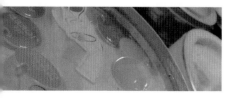

applause:
"Dunic has an eye for flirty little French-inspired clothes for women and favours loads of local designers..."
- vancouver magazine

motherland clothing

2539 main street. between west broadway and ???
604-876-0??0. www.motherlandclothing.com. info@motherlandclothing.com
m-tw & ss???1??m-??pm, th & f 11am-7pm, su noon-?pm

cute and inexpensive clothing and accessories for men and women
opened in 1999. owner: lawrence sampson
amex. mc. visa. debit. jcb
january and july seasonal sales

> *s25*

for the fashion-challenged among us, this fun and hip spot can put some sizzle back in your wardrobe. for years lawrence has stocked motherland with whimsical and comfortable clothing created by canadian designers. his own humorous take on the fashion scene is also in evidence throughout the store. i for one love the motherland t-shirts.

covet:
motherland trousers for men & women
original motherland screen-printed t-shirts
gravis bags & shoes
clothing by oona, parc & togs designs
jewellery by yums designs & sandpaper
lomography bags & camera accessories

53

narcissist design co.

women's clothing boutique featuring the narcissist collection of dresses and seperates
opened in 1997. owner: sara robson francoeur
amex. mc. visa. debit
semi-annual $50-off coupon sale in january and july

> **s26**

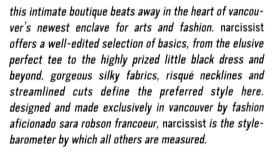

this intimate boutique beats away in the heart of vancouver's newest enclave for arts and fashion. narcissist offers a well-edited selection of basics, from the elusive perfect tee to the highly prized little black dress and beyond. gorgeous silky fabrics, risqué necklines and streamlined cuts define the preferred style here. designed and made exclusively in vancouver by fashion aficionado sara robson francoeur, narcissist *is the style-barometer by which all others are measured.*

covet:
our seasonal LBD (little black dress!)
a sexy top cut long in the body to wear with jeans
simple a-line skirt with unique appliques
64 styles of narcissist made to order t's

applause:
"Hands-down best dresses!"
- vancouver sun

object design gallery

1551 johnston street. east of the public market. net creekhouse
604 681 9977. www.objectdesigngallery.com. objects1@telus.net
daily. 10am - 6pm

jewellery, art, accessories, diamonds
opened in 1996. owners: tamara clark and sako khatcherian
amex. mc. visa
jewellery exhibitions by international artists every four months

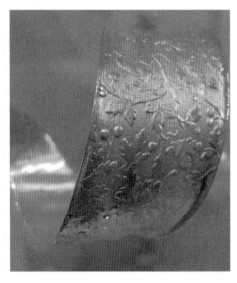

as cool as it can be to travel the world hunting for rare and unique treasures, some striking works can be had right here at home. object design gallery *specializes in the works of canadian jewelery designers; it started with five lines and now features over a hundred. every case has something wonderful tucked into it. you can get lost in the possibilities of this place.*

covet:
engagement rings & wedding bands
  custom-designed by master goldsmith sako
jewellery from over 100 canadian artists
enamelled torso neckpiece by tamara clark
john blair's sea blue chalcedony collection
crocheted sterling silver jewellery by tess klein

about:
"Housing the most diverse and exciting wearable art in Canada."

oceandrive leather

leather garments and accessories
opened in 1998. owners: darryl and keith christensen
amex. mc. visa. debit

> s28

set in an assiduously hip neighborhood that has emerged out of-what else?-a dusty old warehouse district, this lush loft offers buttery soft leather jackets, hot skirts and suede bikinis in a spirit of less is more. the leather itself is spanish or italian, but the results are hand-crafted right across the street.

covet:
sexy fitted jackets
hip-hugging leather pants
ultrasoft suedes
warm, cozy shearling coats
skirts in varying shapes & lengths

they say:
"We have fashioned jackets and pants for many celebrities including Angelina Jolie, Ben Affleck, Christian Slater, and Eddie Murphy."

59

paperhaus

contemporary presentation, organization and storage materials
owners: matthew crossin and dean curley
amex. mc. visa. debit

> *s29*

some of us still have that residual fascination with buying school supplies; it it really was the best part of a new school year. paperhaus is cleverly disguised: it looks like a store, carrying sleekly engineered pens, portfolios and bags, but what owners dean and matt really have created is a home for stationery and organization fetishists. I envision not just my desk becoming a model of clean lines and notes written in perfect penmanship but my entire home. (though even just a supremely organized desk would be a triumph.)

covet:

rexite multiplor (spinning desk catch all)
mac jacket by nava (a wetsuit for your workbook)
studium by naya (world's most beautiful
  letter tray)
3 up by naya (all your books in one)
ego backpack by naya (everyone wants one)

paper-ya

purveyors of beautiful papers and treasures from around the world
opened in 1986. owners: denise carson wilde and sharyn yuen
mc. visa. debit

> s30

if there is an occasion that warrants a card, **paper-ya** is my first and last destination. if there is a parcel that needs to be wrapped and ribboned, off i go to **paper-ya**. no other shop makes me giddy at the prospect of riffling through it - and through the layers upon layers of textured sheets of woven paper, reams of brilliant vellum and delicate tissue. there is always something new to uncover - handsome tins of bronzed italian paper clips, leather-bound journals from florence, hand-dyed ribbons, well, enough said. surely someone's birthday is on the horizon.

covet:
laugh out loud cards
gorgeous invitation cards
retro 51 pens
pinetti wood photo albums
japanese chiogami

applause:
"What a great store!" - daily customer exclamation

63

pigeon

227 carrall street. south of cordova
604.899.6025. www.pigeonshop.ca. info@pigeonshop.ca
tu - sa. 11am - 6pm. su. m. 12pm - 5pm

vancouver-exclusive purveyors of high end streetwear, art, books
opened in 2003. owners: denny lee and neil simonton
amex. mc. visa. debit

pigeon > **s31**

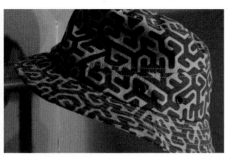

pigeon *has a stubbornly unique sense of style. co-owner denny lee says he likes the grit at his end of the gastown neighbourhood, and his customers don't mind going out of their way in search of* pigeon's *artist-centric clothing. these guys have a devotion to a global urban lifestyle, and they have tracked down rare and special goods from small labels around the world.*

covet:
yoko devereaux
zakee shariff
ju$t another rich kid
our staff
installations
art

65

pleasant girl

647.877.XXXX www.pleasantgirl.com info@pleasantgirl.com

girly streetwear and feminine officewear from independent canadian designers
opened in 2003. owner: lawrence sampson
mc. visa. debit

> *s32*

this free-spirited, feminine boutique is replete with glam clothes that translate well from work to weekend. a sweet girly nuance is woven through most of the labels, many of them designed and manufactured in canada. cute panties, fanciful jewellery, and plenty of pink: let's enjoy being a girl.

covet:
flats & kitten-heeled shoes by irregular choice
everything by geek boutique, especially the pants
astrosatchel vinyl applique bags & accessories
gentle fawn's sporty & feminine tops
sterling silver & bubble-inspired jewellery
cute, sexy undies

applause:
"Its true happy place lies with girly clothing and cheeky add-ons." - flare magazine

67

readerwear

place. 80 water street. vancouver. v6b 1a4. canada. 604.765.1955
1918 maple stree. vancouver. v6j 3s4. canada. 604.922.2925
www.readerwear.com. www.myreaderwear.com
mon. sat. 10am - 6pm. sun. noon - 5pm

stylish ready-to-wear reading glasses
— opened in 2001. owner: wayne yarrow
mc. visa. debit

eyewear > **s33**

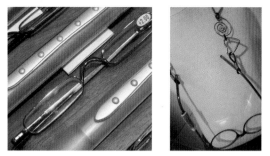

to hell with bifocals - this funky shrine to funkified eyewear is layered in sleek displays of cool reading glasses (even if those latter three words sound a bit like an oxymoron). leopard-print cases safeguard these terribly stylish gems, and dakota, as devoted a saleswoman as you'll find, will happily model an assortment of her latest favs. well, the first twenty or so, anyway.

covet:
teensy-weensy reading glasses
sun readers
sax flexi lites
retroesque designs by nyc's corrine mccormack

assertion:
"Readerwear will change the way you feel about reading glasses."

ric yuenn

special occasion dresses tailored to taste and fit
opened in 1992. owner: ric yuen
amex. mc. visa
january sale

gastown > *s34*

the moment you stroll into this serene little shop, you will be torn between two lovers competing for your attention: the alluring bustiers in vivid hues of fresh green and aubergine; and elegant asian-style dresses with au courant mandarin collars. evening bags reminiscent of the 1920s could almost adorn either ensemble. spend a few minutes shuffling through and you are bound to find a dress you adore, in a colour you love.

ric likes:
brocade silks
satin stretch anything
dresses with low-pleated backs
dresses with plunging fronts

71

richard kidd

115 water street. between cambie and carrall
604.687.1930 www.richardkidd.com / richardrichardkidd.net
mon - sat: 10am - 6pm. su & holidays: noon - 5pm

luxury clothing and accessories boutique
opened in 2004. owner: raif adelberg and caterina scrivano
all major credit cards accepted
boxing day sale & twice yearly seasonal sales

gastown **>** *s35*

okay, this guy stole my dream design for the ultimate apartment and then installed an otherworldly, cool clothing store inside it. raif adelberg has created a place so striking that it can distract you from the unique duds that inhabit it. richard kidd strains from the extraordinary, designs worn by few and seldom recognized by everyone else: libertine, lucien pellat-finet and more.

covet:
carpe diem
comme des garçons
junya watanabe
libertine
lucien pellat-finet
martin margiela
number (n)ine

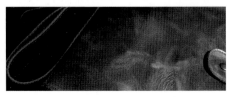

so they say:
"I want to give the shopper an experience they aren't accustomed to."
- raif adelberg

73

robert held art glass

2130 b ... ... vancouver bc, and th
604 737 0020. www.robertheld.com. info@robertheld.com
m ... sa. noon-6 pm. su. noon-5pm.

decorative art glass
opened in 1978. owner: robert held
mc. visa. debit
scratch and dent sale in april and christmas sale in late november/early december

kitsilano > *s36*

a lot of sound and fury goes into the creation of delicate and intricate art glass. the fury comes from the furnaces that roar in robert held's hot shop. the sound, strangely enough, seems to come from loud dance music... at least when I was there. somehow the beat adds to the fantastic quality of the fragile wares that adorn the adjacent gallery.

covet:
cylinder peacock vases
the extra extra large elements pot
gold iris-footed flower vases inspired by feinstein
silver-green mini paperweights

more about:
Robert Held was commissioned to create a gift worthy of Queen Elizabeth II's Golden Jubilee visit to Canada.

75

room 430

430 hornet street, sicily, south of pender
604.805.0353. room430@mail.ai
m..sa..10am..6am..su..1pm..5pm

fashion forward clothing and accessories, new and used records
opened in 2004. owners: dawn archer, lisa osei and desmond niles
mc. visa. debit. jcb

> *s37*

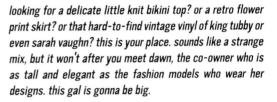

looking for a delicate little knit bikini top? or a retro flower print skirt? or that hard-to-find vintage vinyl of king tubby or even sarah vaughn? this is your place. sounds like a strange mix, but it won't after you meet dawn, the co-owner who is as tall and elegant as the fashion models who wear her designs. this gal is gonna be big.

covet:
azool handmade accessories
record exchange in soul, jazz, funk, rnb
sexy hand-painted t-shirts by azool
one-of-a-kind tweed blend suiting by lisa osei
girly girl vintage-inspired dresses
anna kosturova's crotcheted bikinis

applause:
"The clothes have a sweet, sexy-girlie style that makes you think of '50s pinups, Roman Holiday, and vintage Barbie outfits". - straight.com. august 2004

77

roost

192 hamilton street. northeast corner of drake and hamilton
604.253.0034 . www.roosthome.com . info@roosthome.com
hrs: sa - 10am - 6pm . su : noon - 5pm

homeware
opened in 2001. owners: cimone and laurie schelle
amex. mc. visa

yaletown **>** **s38**

style and delight reverberate off the sturdy beams, exposed brick walls and high ceilings that make up roost. in a compendium of delightful works from canada, australia and scandanavia, whimsical plume-studded purses and "love" plates, almost too delicate and too distinct to eat off of, vie with tiny cubes of resin, glass, ceramic and silver for fleur de sel and pepper rubs. laurie and cimone are almost certain to have the prized pair of earrings you can't bear to live without.

covet:
warm tea set by tonfisk
vibrant handmade pieces from dinosaur design
joy bags in all prints & fabrics
chocolate satin-glazed bottles by elliot golightly

motto:
"Concerned with the nesting habits of humans."

sate

1736 west 10th avenue. between granville and fir
604.731.5558 www.satgimports.com sate@telus.net
m-sa 10-5.30 pm sidewalk su neon zero

unique and functional home décor, furniture and fashion & café
opened in 2002. owners: lorne tyczenski and stephen greenham
mc. visa. debit

south granville > *s39*

i love it when synergy works: at sate you can quaff your cappuccino while shopping for treasures hand-picked by lorne and stephen during their extensive travels in the far east. thai silks, embroidered handbags and an eclectic assortment of ornate ceramics are part of the lingua franca here. sumptuous silk kimonos hang alongside baskets brimming with textured obis, beaded and embroidered handbags. each piece is special and tasteful.

covet:
colourful & multi-functional lacquer bowls
silk lamps to induce romance
elegant saltwater cultured pearls
vietnamese coffee
silk kimonos, shawls & wraps in vibrant shades

small | medium | large

604.6.... www........com.....@....ca

canadian contemporary furniture, objects, art and design
opened in 2002. owner: david hepworth
amex. mc. visa

> *s40*

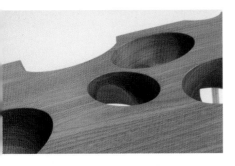

david has designed a space that is minimalist, functional and simply wonderful. my dream apartment is almost entirely furnished with pieces from this shop. a low-rise coffee table will seat several of my friends for an evening of take-away curry. or perhaps i'll opt for the desk that doubles as a perfect dining table. sculptured wooden bowls and lamps as objets d'art vie for your attention. whatever your desire, this place has it in your size.

covet:
gailan ngan pottery
david greig gallery bench in hemlock
fastback sofa bed designed by steve suchy
derek young tables

something blue

bridal shop featuring designer wedding gowns and bridesmaid dresses
opened in 1997. owners: heather lewis and jija park
mc. visa. interac. cheque

downtown > **s41**

although i'm not the marrying kind, the promise of a shopping expedition to something blue might be enough to soften my resolve. especially if it means entrusting heather and jija with the design of my wedding dress. their tastes reflect a west coast sensibility - beautiful, elegant and understated-and, happily ever after, not a single poofy, meringue gown is in sight.

covet:
something blue private label gowns
vera wang gowns
regina b. jewelry & accessories
vera wang evening gown line

applause:
Our vision is to do what we do so well that people will feel inspired to tell others about Something Blue

85

spank on the drive

contemporary women's clothing
opened in 2002. owner: jana sehic and ron kerr
mc. visa. debit
major sales in january and july
special event in june: canadian fashion awareness month

> *s42*

picture it: an uncommon shop in a wide open space in a neighbourhood that defies description. sexy, slitted and saucy pieces tart up the walls. a bright orange sofa anchors the room. spank screams hard-core edgy outfits for women who love to be noticed. browse awhile while jana stands at the ready to answer, outfit and exalt.

covet:
japanese influenced dresses with a modern twist
asymmetrical spider-web sweaters from london
deconstructed t-shirts by full circle designs
alison wonderland jackets
streetwear from the people have spoken designs
asymmetrical neck tops from kitchen orange
retro inspired dresses from spank private label

so they say:
"Our customers are women who like clothing with soul and expression."

87

spiral living decor

3030 granville street. across street at 15th.
604.730.2566 www.spiralliving.com info@spiralliving.com
m - sat. 10am - 5:30pm. sun. 11am - 5pm

selected home décor from france
opened in 1997. owners: blair and noriko zimmerman
mc. visa

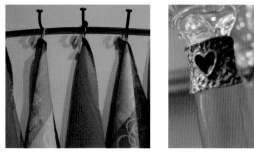

when i walk into this store a church-like stillness envelops me. this temple is devoted to beautiful, modern fabrics, and it is brimming with fancy rugs and fine cloth. blair and noriko buy some tasteful things, attractive talismans in the pursuit of accessible modernism.

covet:
serge lesage carpets
trendy washable rugs
colourful & classic jacquard tablecloths
bedding in quality egyption cotton
contemporary italian sofas

89

still life interiors

fine furniture gallery specializing in custom, handcrafted solid wood furniture
opened in 1999. owners: john yamazaki and ellen fairn
amex. mc. visa. debit

> **s44**

imagine a world where furniture doesn't come from some scandinavian factory or require any assembly. in this world, all your furniture has beautiful wood grain and is so steady, so well made and so elegant that it's clear that any rocking is the floor's fault. and every piece you buy becomes an heirloom. this is what john yamazaki and ellen fairn have created at still life interiors. this year my piggy bank is dedicated to a side table. next year, maybe, i'll get the sleigh bed.

covet:
the cherry sleighbed built locally by hand
handcrafted solid walnut dining chairs
glass lattice coffee table
all of our solid wood one-of-a-kind custom pieces

they say:
"Quality has no compromise! Committed to classic design, quality materials and time-honoured craftsmanship, Still Life provides custom home furnishings for life."

ta da!

vintage and european chic furniture and accessories
opened in 2000. owner: lauree duprey-reed
amex. mc. visa. debit

> **s45**

this is european chic on a busy street, a bustling path that traverses nearly the entire lower mainland from west to east. apart from a stray coffee shop nearby, it stands alone in location and sensibility. the colours are so comforting here: striped pink tapered candles, throw pillows in robin's eggshell blue, cotton candy pink glassware, comfy cocoa fauteuils. ta da! is a cushy, chromatic wonderland.

covet:
mariage frères tea from france
eclectic vintage furniture & lighting
eskandar bath & body products from england
vintage cotton linen pillows with sheer buttons
silver jewellery designed by parisian artisans

tenthirteight

1026 mainland street. between nelson and davie
604.669.6469 | www.t38.com. mail@t38.ca
m - thu 11am - 6pm. fri 11am - 7pm. sat. noon - 6pm .su. 2pm - 5pm

urban streetwear for those in the know
opened in 1994. owner: glyn roberts
amex. mc. visa. debit

> *s46*

tenthirtyeight has barely created even a ripple of buzz among the locals, which is just fine by this story's quiet but loyal following. local tech workers, japanese exchange students and young actors looking for a breakthrough in hollywood north populate this place. It's the favourite day-after-wear for all those sunglasses-adorned cool kids hunched over an iced latte and trying to conjure up the events of the night before.

covet:
levi's premium
150 styles of tees
special edition nike shoes
anything by arc'teryx
bags for school & work
stussy stuff

the cross decor & design

1198 homer street. corner of davie and homer
604.689.2900 www.thecrossdesign.com thecrossdesign@telus.net
m - sa. 10am - 6pm. su. 12pm - 5pm

vintage, modern home furnishings and accessories
opened in 2003. owners: darci ilich and stephanie vogler
amex. mc. visa. debit

religious artifacts aren't much in evidence here, despite the solemn name of this home-décor store. but the cross does offer a sanctuary of its own, in a cavernous and well-lit space that is a tranquil hideaway from the noisy street that runs past it. on every visit i work hard to resist sinking into the cushy chocolate sofa that beckons from a corner of the room, freeing up more time to browse among the quilted bed throws, pillows trimmed in blue piping, tapered candles and a mosaic of fabrics and silk ribbons. i never really need any of this, and that's the point.

covet:
exclusive bedding & custom pillows
caramel leather cigar chairs
parisian crystal chandeliers
original paintings by local artists
fluffy lambskin rugs

applause:
"The Cross has mastered the mix, pairing soft vintage with budding modern, and home-grown with European."
- canadian house & home

97

the natural gardener garden store

garden store and nursery
opened in 2003. owner: bob tuckey
amex. mc. visa. debit

> *s48*

i suffer from garden envy. bob's natural gardener *is a place that pushes me to my limits. he has gone out of his way to procure plants no one else can get; when i asked to see the carnivorous pitcher plant in action-shades of "little shop of horrors"!-he proudly complied. "these are all full of wasps," he said. yum, or ewww. but either way, cool.*

covet:
glass frog pot perchers
wall flower limited edition prints
petit fleur bucket vases
orchids
slate vases by john quinn of saltspring island
polemonium snow & sapphire

99

woofgang

pet supplies and accessories
opened in 2003. owners: raymond chang and mark chung
amex. mc. visa. debit

> **s49**

eating at **wild rice** *is a lot like meeting a celebrity you've had a crush on for a while: your expectations are exceeded.* **wild rice** *is taller and more attractive in person. parked on the edge of vancouver's chinatown, it shows why gastronomes around the city have fallen in love with the moderne chinese cuisine (i long for the long beans). a bonus: at night, the beautiful people haunt the bar, hungry for its sexy vibe.*

imbibe:
house-infused vodka

devour:
kung po chicken with house-spiced peanuts
shiitake dusted triple-a beef tenderloin
warm chinese greens & edamame salad
pan-seared pacific halibut

applause:
"Wild Rice is the consummate millennial opium den - the opiates replaced with vodka drinks at the centre ice bar, the opium dreams with plated fantasies brought to earth."
- jamie maw, vancouver magazine

103